Stephanie Lisa Tara's

Turtle Book

fotos, facts, and fun!

written by **Stephanie Lisa Tara**

flip book by **Lee Edward Födi**

End

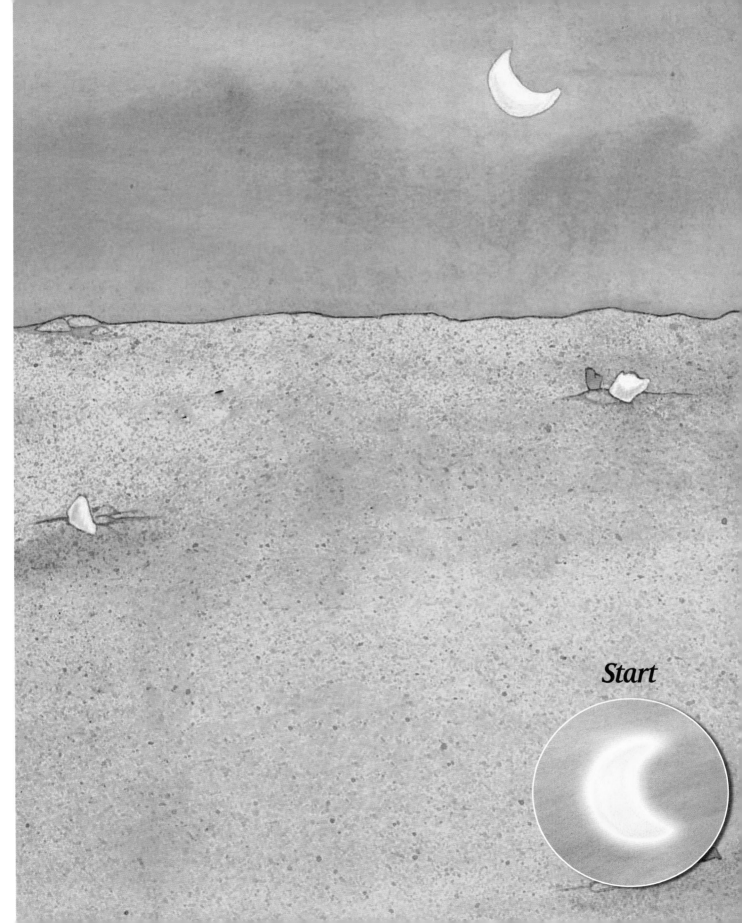

Start

Preserve. Conserve. Inspire. Teach.

Stephanie Lisa Tara
CHILDREN'S BOOKS

© 2013 Stephanie Lisa Tara
Original illustrations by Lee Edward Födi
Edited by Josey Gist
Layout and design by Ted Ruybal
No toxic materials were used in the manufacturing of this book.

Stephanie Lisa Tara's Turtle Book

Stephanie Lisa Tara Children's Books
1 Blackfield Drive Box #312
Tiburon, CA 94920

Preserve. Conserve. Inspire. Teach.

ISBN-13: 978-0-9894334-5-7
LCCN: 2011929050

Printed in the United States
10 9 8 7 6 5 4 3 21 0

For more information about the author, or the book,
please visit: www.stephanielisatara.com.

ABOUT

Author

Stephanie Lisa Tara I've always believed that magic hides in special places. As a child, people would often stare at my bright red hair, which was very, very bright indeed. Unfortunately, I developed a bad habit of making up rhymes about all of them, and they soon became funny characters. I didn't have much time to think about being different; fanciful lyricisms danced in my head, and no one was safe!

Since then, I've come to believe that storytelling has the power to inspire a deep love of language and learning. Words tripping off the tongue in somersaults that stick to your thoughts like taffy—those are the things that stay forever in the mind. I've lived in many special places: on a farm, in a city skyscraper, on a tropical beach, and in the beautiful country of France.

Now I live in northern California, between the redwood forests and the sea. Even though I'm an adult, I'm still as silly as ever. Many nice words have been used to describe my books, such as fun, engaging, delightful, and whimsical. Some folks say that I deliver timeless messages of love for kids and parents to share again and again; this makes me very happy. I hope that you'll enjoy my stories, too. Captivating children with language is something that I believe in, and I strive to live my life with this always.

Illustrator

Lee Edward Födi has been writing and illustrating stories about all sorts of animals for as long as he can remember. Growing up on a farm, he was inspired by the company of countless creatures—hamsters, cats, dogs, parakeets, rabbits, frogs turtles, newts, and his very first pet: a blind and ruffled old hen. Many things have changed since his boyhood days, but Lee's love of nature has not. He currently lives and works on the west coast of Canada, where he enjoys an abundance of nature and the steady array of critters that frequent his neighborhood. Visit his web-site at www.leefodi.com.

Editor

Josey Gist is a British writer, editor and blogger with a passion for satirical fantasy and science fiction novels, animation, and animal rights. She is the founder of A Wrinkle in the Pages, a blog all about teen fantasy books and movies. She has a MA in Archaeology for Screen Media, and loves to visit historical buildings and museums. Josey lives and writes in El Cerrito, California, where she spends most of her time with her creative husband and bossy cat. Keep in touch with josey on Twitter or follow her blog at: www.awrinkleinthepages.com.

TABLE OF CONTENTS

PROLOGUE

A Personal Note from Stephanie Lisa Turtle (Okay, Tara)

Dear Turtle Activists,

I want to thank each and every one of you for your tireless dedication and love to our cause! I have written this book FOR YOU! I dedicate this book TO YOU! **120 pages of fotos, facts and fun!**

Stephanie Lisa Tara's Turtle Book has a primary goal: **SAVING SEA TURTLES FROM EXTINCTION**. A portion of proceeds from this book go to charitable organizations like the Turtle Foundation (www.turtle-foundation.org) of whom my first turtle book, I'LL FOLLOW THE MOON—is a proud sponsor.

If you are new to us—please join with us, for together, holding hands, we can effect change. Yes—really! xoxo. SAVE GREEN SEA TURTLES on Facebook (www.facebook.com/.../Save-Green-Sea-Turtles/33363600998) is our hugely popular hangout—tens of thousands of Activists-strong. Please join us!

NOW—prepare for something totally new and amazing!

Stephanie Lisa Tara's Turtle Book is not your typical scientific turtle book: my special book is all about having **FUN!** Enjoy the mini **FLIP-BOOK** in the corners and create a movie of your own! Click the ebook pages—or thumb through manually in the paperback—YOUR CHOICE!

I've written these chapters in a fun, chatty voice—you know, the one YOU use when talking up your favorite topics! Don't be surprised if you find yourself giggling as you turn pages! Enjoy breathtaking photography, incredible facts, and way-out wow'ing surprises that these millennium-old creatures have to share.

AND: **TWO IS BETTER THAN ONE!** Yep! **Stephanie Lisa Tara's Turtle Book** is my second turtle book—it's a perfect TWIN to my first international bestseller, I'LL FOLLOW THE MOON: buy BOTH TOGETHER for your shelf. **Two little twins; one a fable, one fotos, facts & fun.**

So, in closing . . . please accept this deeply personal gift from me, your faithful **sea turtle leader,** the **turtle-lady,** or **Stephanie Lisa Turtle**—as I was renamed recently by a fan—from my heart to yours.

God bless everyone who has supported the cause
to save sea turtles from extinction!

Chapter One

So, Stephanie, WHY sea turtles?

OMG: I'm asked this question all the time!

And it's true—I'm **enchanted** with sea turtles. And it all happened quite by accident, really. I am not a scientist, I don't even scuba dive. All I did was have a baby. 'Huh?', you may ask yourselves. Did she give birth to a sea turtle? Well, no, not exactly.

But I did give birth to a human child and on the night I brought her home from the hospital—I noticed something quite strange on the beach in front of our south Florida home. It was late and I was tired, doing a last-one-of-the-day bottle feeding on the deck after a long day of new mom activities. As Maddie slurped down the final ounce of her formula with that familiar glup, glup, glup sound, I noticed dark, tiny shapes scurrying across the sand. What was this? I wondered and went down for a closer look.

There they were! **BABY SEA TURTLES** streaming out of hundreds of small nests; gentle rises in the sand were their markers. The babies made fanciful patterns in the sand as they dashed on little green legs in a remarkable race to the sea. I watched them hop, one by one, into welcoming waves that sparkled under the beautiful moonlight. **"I'm coming Mama . . ."** they seemed to be saying, and I realized that I was witnessing one of nature's sacred events, the love bond between mother and child. It is this precious feeling that inspired me to write 'I'll Follow the Moon', that came into being a few years later. Nobody was more surprised than I when this little turtle book became an international bestseller.

One thing led to another, as often happens in life. I started a community cause page about sea turtles on Facebook.

And—thousands of people joined. I was stunned. We laughed, we cried, we applauded—the turtles were so entertaining, indeed, they were inspiring. But they are something else too: **endangered**. For a hundred million years they've prospered here on earth, and now they are on the verge of extinction.

It is this premise that occupies my mind. And this is why I've taken up the torch to save them. Please enjoy this book as a gift from me to you, and all I ask you to do is spread the word about our friends, the sea turtles. As old as time, they've always symbolized survival against all odds, and they are now facing their most courageous battle yet: **EXTINCTION**. Remember folks, extinction is forever . . . so, I'm asking you to please help!

Proceeds from the sale of this book are being donated to charitable organizations that pledge to return sea turtles to prosperity.

Thank you and blessings,
Stephanie Tara

All eight species of sea turtles are listed as threatened or endangered on the U.S. Endangered and Threatened Wildlife and Plants List. It is illegal to harm, or in any way interfere with, a sea turtle or its eggs.

- **Green Sea Turtle**
- **Black Sea Turtle**
- **Leatherback Sea Turtle**
- **Loggerhead Sea Turtle**
- **Hawksbill Sea Turtle**
- **Kemp's Ridley Sea Turtle**
- **Olive Ridley Sea Turtle**
- **Flatback Sea Turtle**

Chapter Two

Hmmm, just what is a SEA TURTLE exactly?

Pay attention! There will be a test! (LOL, only kidding) . . . but really

A sea turtle is a MARINE REPTILE. They have been on the earth since the time of the dinosaurs, 200 million years ago! The very first ancestral sea turtle's name was a mouthful: Odontochelys. (pronunciation guide). Life at that time was dangerous—full of predators, so the sea turtle had to evolve to protect itself: its SHELL was the perfect answer! Just think how much safer YOU would feel—if YOU had a SHELL! You could avoid being a target for paper airplanes, for example. Or projectile books, if you have a particularly nasty teacher. Sea turtles are different from all other turtles in that they have a specially shaped shell designed for swimming . . . they cannot retract their head and limbs into their shells either. They have flippers which are like paddles that help them move quickly in the warm seas they enjoy. Kind of like human arms and legs.

Most scientists recognize eight species of sea turtles, and have assigned fancy Latin names to them:

1. Green *Chelonia mydas*
2. Black (also know as Eastern Pacific green turtle) *Chelonia agassizii*
3. Loggerhead *Caretta caretta*
4. Hawksbill *Eretmochelys imbricata*
5. Leatherback *Dermochelys coriacea*
6. Kemp's ridley *Lepidochelys kempii*
7. Olive ridley *Lepidochelys olivacea*
8. Flatback *Natator depressus*

Chapter Three

INSIDE and OUTSIDE a sea turtle, innards, guts, & stuff.

What, you think you are the only ones who have skin covering your icky inside stuff ? Wrong!

All sea turtles, except the leatherback, have both an internal and external skeleton. The sea turtle's external skeleton provides support and protection for internal organs and is comprised of the upper **carapace** (the shell on their back) and the lower **plastron** (the shell on their belly). The internal skeleton provides an anchor for the turtles' muscles. Again, with the exception of the leatherback, the turtle's spine is fused (like glue) to his or her carapace.

The **flippers** are large and very sensitive. The front flippers are like propellers generating speed; the rear flippers are like rudders, providing both direction and stability to the turtles' movement. Turtles are a lot like small but heavy, powerful paddle boats. The flippers are also used by females to dig the egg cavity during nesting.

Sea turtles have **no teeth!** Instead, their mouths are sharp, **beak-like** and well-suited for crushing or tearing their food. A leatherback's mouth contains a series of backward pointing spines that prevent jellyfish from slipping back into the water.

Sea turtles **eyes** give them great underwater vision, but are not so useful on land where they give the turtle a *very* near-sighted view of our world. (No, they can't wear glasses!) When females are on land a gland releases salty fluids to keep their eyes moist, and help them get rid of the excess salt they ingest when drinking sea water. That's why female turtles shed tears while laying their nests. Legend has it that the Mother is crying for its unborn young, but science provides us with a more logical answer.

Sea turtles do not have **ears!** But they *are* capable of perceiving low frequency **sounds and vibrations.** One of the turtle's most powerful attributes is its **sense of smell.** This robust sniffer seems to help them return to the beach where they were hatched in order to create a nest and lay their own eggs! Imagine a human remembering the smell of the hospital or other place they were born in. And then finding it in a far-off country with only the help of their nose!

One obvious distinction among turtles is the size of their **tails!** Female's tails are short and do not extend beyond the hind flippers. However, male tails are considerably larger, often extending well past their hind limbs. So if you need to spot the difference, remember to look at a sea turtle's tail length. Only the female has an *ovipositor*, the structure used to deposit her eggs.

(The spine of the leatherback is not fused with its carapace, nor does it have a bony shell. Instead, it is covered with a leathery skin supported by an array of tiny bones. These adaptations allow it to dive up to *three thousand* feet below the surface, where tremendous water pressure would crush a less flexible body.)

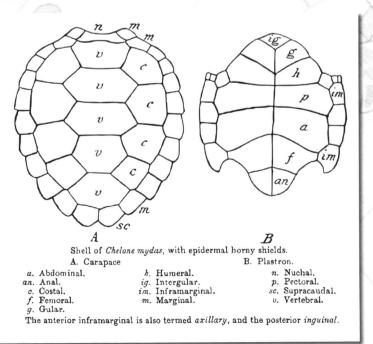

Shell of *Chelone mydas*, with epidermal horny shields.

A. Carapace   B. Plastron.

a. Abdominal.   *h.* Humeral.   *n.* Nuchal.
an. Anal.   *ig.* Intergular.   *p.* Pectoral.
c. Costal.   *im.* Inframarginal.   *sc.* Supracaudal.
f. Femoral.   *m.* Marginal.   *v.* Vertebral.
g. Gular.

The anterior inframarginal is also termed *axillary*, and the posterior *inguinal*.

Chapter Four

Sea turtle senses:
HEAR, SEE, TOUCH, TASTE & SMELL

Yes indeed, you bet your flippers that sea turtles know what's going on around them!

HEARING:

All reptiles, including sea turtles, have a single bone in the middle ear that conducts vibrations to the inner ear. Imagine headphones permanently fused to your inner ear. Researchers have found that sea turtles respond to low frequency sounds and vibrations. So they can hear things that we can't.

EYESIGHT:

Sea turtles can see well under water but are shortsighted in the air. Under experimental conditions, loggerhead and green sea turtle hatchlings exhibited a preference for near-ultraviolet, violet, and bluegreen light. Their vision allows them to spot their prey when swimming around.

TOUCH:

A sea turtle is sensitive to touch on the soft parts of its flippers and on its shell. So don't be tempted to tickle a turtle!

TASTE:

At this point, very little is known about a sea turtle's sense of taste. For example, is it able to taste what it's eating the way you or I would savor chocolate? And would it enjoy ice cream? (This is unlikely.)

SMELL:

Most researchers believe that sea turtles have a strong sense of smell in the water. Experiments show that hatchlings react to the scent of shrimp, and it is why I strongly recommend not wearing shrimp-scented perfume while scuba diving, unless you want to be nibbled to death by tiny turtles. This affinity for shrimp helps them to locate food in murky water. A sea turtle draws in water through the nose then immediately empties the water out again through the mouth. This pulsating movement is thought to be associated with smelling, and makes drinking soda impossible, although luckily, sea turtles don't like soda.

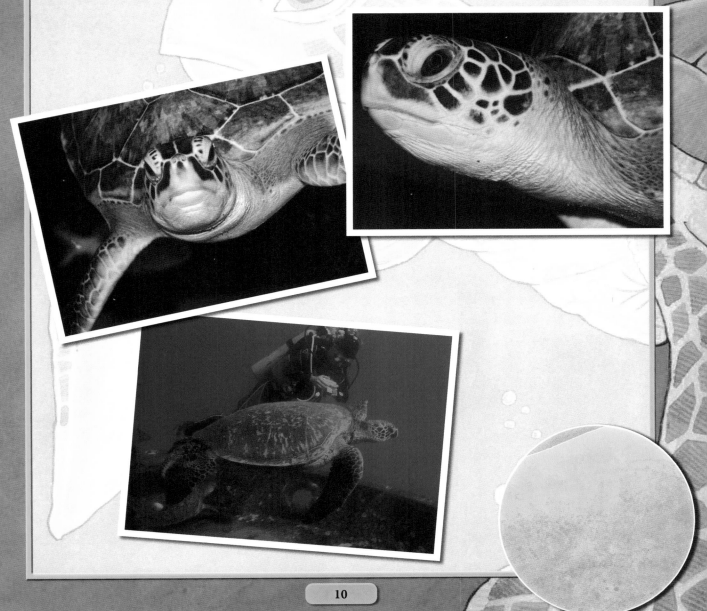

Chapter Five

HOW in the underwater world does a sea turtle BREATHE?

OKAY, DEEP BREATH EVERYONE:
sea turtles are truly the most incredible breathers!

Sea turtles are almost always submerged (under the waves), and therefore have developed an anaerobic system of energy metabolism. Anaerobic respiration is a form of respiration using electron acceptors other than oxygen. This means that turtles don't always need oxygen to breathe, which is why turtles are much better at swimming than humans.

Although all sea turtles breathe air, under dire circumstances they may divert to anaerobic metabolism for long periods of time. (Much longer than you can hold your breath underwater.)

When surfacing to breathe, a sea turtle can quickly refill its lungs with a single explosive exhalation and then rapid inhalation. Their large lungs have adapted to permit rapid exchange of oxygen and to avoid trapping gases during deep dives, which can be lethal to humans, and probably quite uncomfortable for turtles.

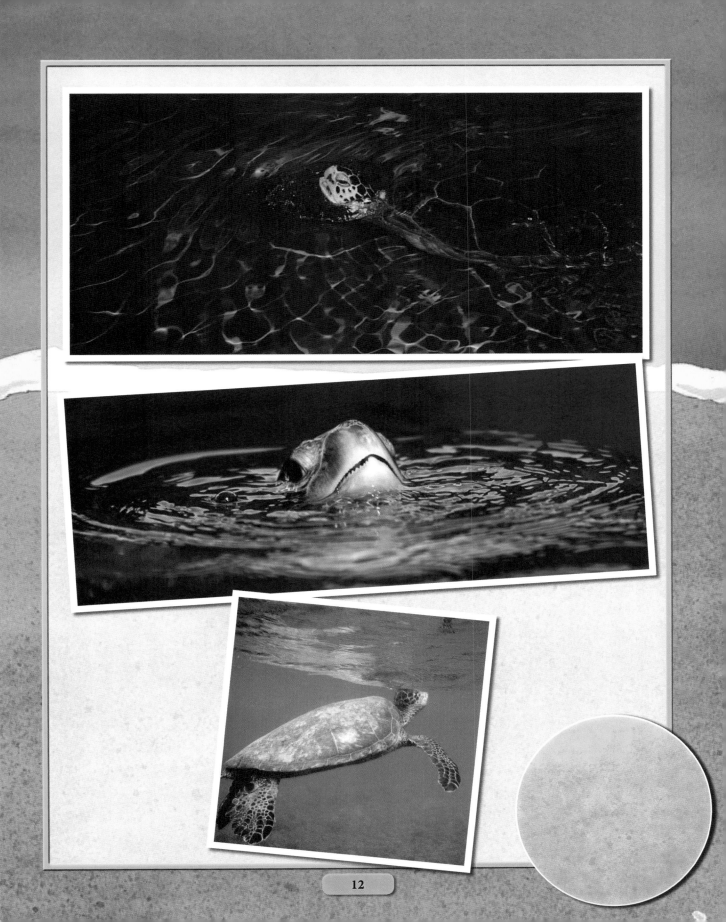

Chapter Six

THE MUNCHIES:
What do sea turtles chomp on?

Did someone say FOOD? Watch out! Here come the turtles!

Sea turtles can dive more than 1,000 feet in order to reach their dinner! But despite this incredible passion for their food, most of the time they remain in shallower water. They are cold blooded so they can dramatically slow down their metabolism. As a result they can go several months without food!

ADULT SEA TURTLE DIET:

Adult **Green** turtles are usually herbivores, like human vegetarians, although hatchlings are omnivores, eating both plants and animals. Their diet consists of algae, sea grasses, and seaweed so they have a serrated, sawlike beak that allows them to scrape algae off rocks and tear up grasses and seaweed. Adult turtles are way more choosy than their offspring, which is weird, because human kids are usually far more picky than adults!

Leatherbacks are sometimes referred to as *gelatinivores* because their diet consists *exclusively* of jellies and other soft-bodied invertebrates like tunicates and sea squirts. Their mouths have two sharply pointed cusps, one on the upper and one on the lower jaw that allows them to pierce jellies and other soft-bodied organisms. Kind of like a vampire turtle, only with cusps instead of fangs. And instead of blood, they really love jellies. Sparkly vampires are no competition for these turtles. They are hungry for popularity (and jellies)!

Adult **Loggerheads** are carnivores, eating only other animals such as crabs, conches, and whelks, while hatchlings are omnivores, eating both plants and animals. Loggerheads have strong jaws so they can crush hard-shelled prey. Tip: don't stick your hand in a loggerhead's mouth. It'll look like all the bones were removed. Floppy. Unpleasant. Not recommended.

Hawksbill are often referred to as *spongivores* because of their specialized diet of almost exclusively sponges. The hawksbill has a sharp, narrow, "bird-like" beak that allows them to reach within crevices on the reef to get their dinner. Poor Spongebob Squarepants - he is this turtle's favorite food!

The **Olive Ridley** is an omnivore, eating a variety of animals and plants including crabs, shrimp, lobster, urchins, jellies, algae, and even fish! Olive Ridley's aren't choosy.

The **Kemp's Ridley** is a carnivore, eating crabs, fish, jellies, shrimp, and a variety of mollusks, but it loves crabs. Crabs, however, aren't sending this turtle any Valentines.

The **Flatback** is an omnivore that consumes sea cucumbers, jellies, soft coral, shrimp, crab, mollusks, fish, and a seaweed salad! I call it the 'fine dining' turtle and imagine it with a bow tie and napkin. And if you really want to remember its name, imagine it laying flat on its back in a restaurant, stuffed full of food!

Chapter Seven

Now, WHERE and HOW do sea turtles like to hang out?

Boy oh boy—do sea turtles know how to hang!

They live in almost EVERY sea around the globe, nesting on tropical and subtropical beaches. But turtles don't just sit on beaches sunbathing, they **migrate long distances** to feed, often crossing entire oceans for a meal! For instance, loggerheads nest in Japan, but migrate to **Baja Mexico** to chow down before heading home (read about Adelita, the first turtle tracked across the Pacific). Turtles are experienced travelers and they like to live it up all over the globe! Now, if only they could tell us all about their adventures . . .

Sea turtles are amazing **swimmers!** They can swim for hours and hours and hours without becoming weary. These speed demons can accelerate from one mile per hour to about five miles per hour! Even at these slow speeds some turtles travel hundreds or even thousands of miles to reach their breeding grounds. This can take a very long time but as everybody knows, slow and steady wins the race!

They are excellent **divers,** in fact leatherbacks can dive up to 3900 feet when in pursuit of a yummy jellyfish snack. Sea turtles are turtle-Olympians when it comes to holding their breath: green sea turtles can make one breath last 5 hours! How do they do this? Their heart rate slows to conserve oxygen; nine minutes may elapse between heartbeats! Before you attempt to break this amazing record, I must warn you that any attempt will result in certain death. We humans are not made for such Olympian breathing techniques!

Are you impressed by sea turtles yet? They are amazing creatures that can do all sorts of things that we puny humans can't even attempt. And just in case you're still feeling superior to the sea turtle . . .

All sea turtles enjoy warm seas, with the exception of the ancient leatherbacks, which are capable of withstanding the coldest water temperatures (often below 40°F BRRRRRR!) and are found as far south as Chile and as far north as Alaska. They spend their entire lives at sea, except when the females come ashore to lay their eggs. This happens several times per season every 2 to 5 years. After about sixty days under the sand, baby sea turtles (known as "hatchlings") emerge and make their way to the shore—attracted to the distant horizon.

The juvenile turtles spend their first few years in open ocean, eventually moving to protected bays, estuaries, and other nearby shore waters. Sort of like humans, who tend to spend most of their adolescence partying in the city, then move to the suburbs as they get older.

Adelita's story: *The journey of Adelita the sea turtle is the true story of a resilient loggerhead sea turtle, wearing a state-of-the-art satellite transmitter, who made her way from Baja California, Mexico to the shores of her birthplace in Japan, some 6,000 miles and 368 days across the Pacific ocean. With no idea if the transmitter would work or where she would go, the team put Adelita into the water on August 10, 1996. Having spent most of her life in small tanks, at first she didn't realize she was free and swam around the outside of the tank. Then she figured it out and disappeared into the Pacific. For almost exactly a year, the young loggerhead made its way west, past Hawaii, eventually reaching the coast of Japan. Her journey measured 9,000 miles, crossing a barren area of ocean that scientists previously believed was a barrier to migration. Amazing!*

Flatback

Kemps Ridley

Olive Ridley

Loggerhead

Green

Leatherback

Chapter Eight

Socialize?
Do sea turtles like to party?

You know how nice it is when you are in your own quiet space swimming around the sea . . . right? Oh! Wait a minute! I forgot, if you're reading this, then you're probably a human. Okay, so maybe you don't know how nice it is, so listen up:

Sea turtles feel like that a lot of the time and so they don't really have big, wild parties together, however, some species do congregate offshore. Of course . . . when it comes time to start dating—sea turtles do get together to **mate**. Members of some species travel together to nesting grounds. At times, when sea turtles feel like taking in some sun, they will be seen basking together atop the sea, like you and your friends at the poolside on a hot day . . . . Olive Ridleys, in fact, often float together by the **thousands** after nesting . . . separate but together, if you know what I mean. But, typically, sea turtles live on their own, spending most of the day feeding and then resting up for the next meal. They can sleep on the surface of the water, or on the bottom! Scuba divers often see turtles napping under rocks and ledges. Scientific tagging and tracking studies have demonstrated that sea turtles often migrate thousands of miles from feeding grounds to breeding grounds! So t h e answer is . . . no, sea turtles don't like to party, generally speaking. They are loners, until they start dating other sea turtles. But they are really, really happy that way.

Chapter Nine

Heading in for the beach:
MAMA! It's time to lay EGGS!

Woah! A mother's job is never done. That goes for all mamas, feathered, furry, and yes—scaly-skinned too!

Sea turtles mate like any other creature does, and then it's time to become a parent! Like other turtles, sea turtles lay eggs. They must come ashore to do so. Females usually nest during the warmest months of the year. The exception is the leatherback turtle, which nests in fall and winter. Females nest a few weeks after mating. Like other turtles, sea turtles come ashore to lay eggs, **and most females return to the same nesting beach each year,** coming ashore at night, alone, most often during high tide. A female sea turtle crawls above the high tide line and, using her front flippers, digs out a "body pit." Then using her hind flippers, she digs an egg cavity. The depth of the cavity is determined by the length of the stretched hind flipper. Imagine only being able to dig a hole that is the exact length of your arm and hand! Without a trowel!

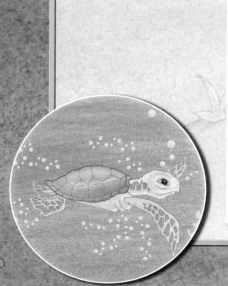

Depending on the species, the female deposits 50 to 200 Ping Pong ball-shaped eggs into the egg cavity. The eggs are soft-shelled, and **are papery to leathery in texture.** They do not break when they fall into the egg cavity. The eggs are surrounded by a thick, clear mucus.

Mama covers the nest with sand using her hind flippers. Burying the eggs serves three purposes: it helps protect the eggs from surface predators who might think of the eggs as a tasty breakfast treat; it helps keep the soft, porous shells moist, thus protecting them from drying out; and it helps the eggs maintain proper temperature. Experts can identify the species of turtle by the type of mound left by the nesting female and by her flipper tracks in the sand. Females may spend two or more hours out of the water during the entire nesting process. Females usually lay between one and nine *clutches* (groups) of eggs per season. That's a lot of baby sea turtles!

The Really Awesome Facts:

Experts can identify the species of turtle by the type of mound left by the nesting female and by her flipper tracks in the sand.

Females may spend two or more hours out of the water during the entire nesting process!

Females usually lay between one and nine *clutches* of eggs per season.

Mother turtles may nest every two to three years.

The Kemp's Ridley and Olive Ridley turtles form up into large groups called *arribadas* (Spanish for "arrival") consisting of thousands of egg-bearing females that come ashore at the exact same time to lay their eggs. The arribadas is a huge nesting party for sea turtles.

Chapter Ten

EGGS: Leathery, funny-looking, but warm!

Hatching and Hatchlings

A. Incubation.

1. Incubation time (how long it takes a collection of baby turtle cells to divide and grow) varies with species, clutch size (how many brothers and sisters the turtle will have), and temperature and humidity in the nest.

2. The incubation time for most species is 45 to 70 days, or only 1.5–2 months!

3. Research indicates that the sex of an embryo is determined sometime after fertilization, as the embryo develops, and may be temperature dependent. Lower nest temperatures produce more males; higher temperatures produce more females.

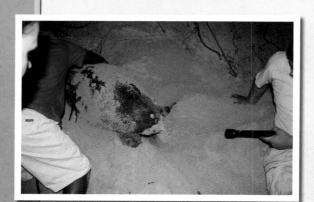

HAWAIIAN GREEN SEA TURTLES
ENJOY THEM FROM A DISTANCE

Sea turtles are protected under State and Federal laws.

PLEASE give turtles space
Sea turtles may come on land to rest.
Please do not disturb or approach turtles.

PLEASE never touch or ride
Sea turtles are wild animals.
Respect and enjoy them from a distance.

PLEASE never feed
Feeding sea turtles will change their natural behavior.
Turtles that learn to associate humans with food
may become aggressive.

Show Turtles Aloha

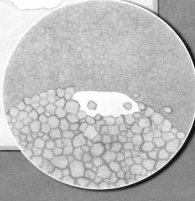

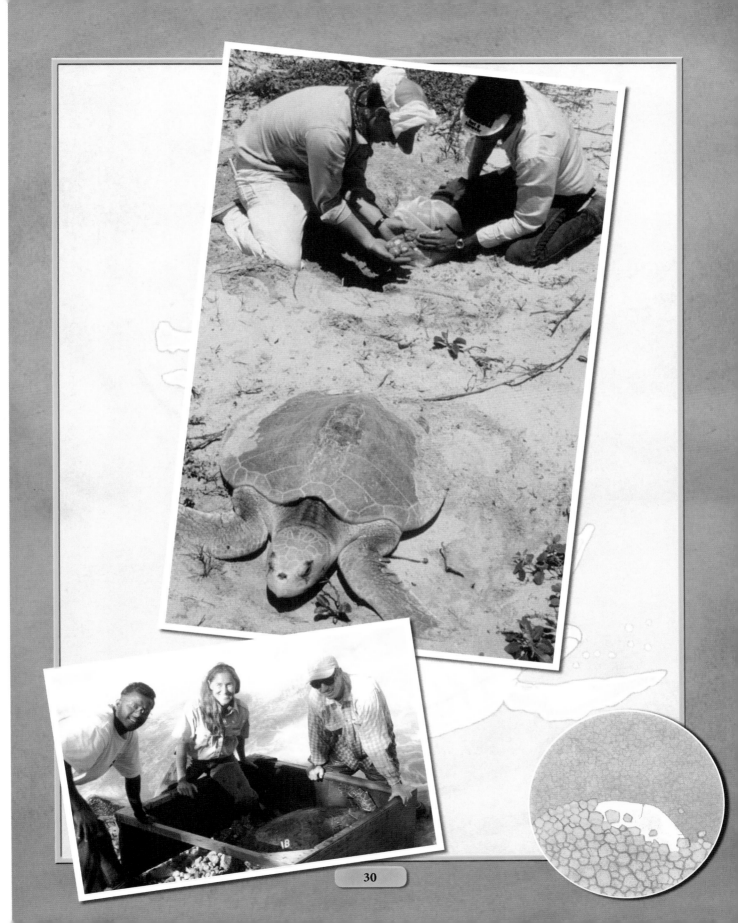

Chapter Eleven

COZY! Three feet under SAND!

B. Hatching.

1. Sea turtles hatch throughout the year but mostly in summer, because, as you know, they are fun-loving creatures who love hitting the beach in summer.

2. Hatchlings use a **caruncle** (temporary egg tooth) to help break open the shell. They have to break out of their shell themselves, with no help. It's hard work being a baby sea turtle!

3. After hatching, the young turtles may take three to seven days to dig their way to the surface.

4. Hatchlings usually wait until night to emerge from the nest. It can be very scary for a baby sea turtle to emerge. Emerging at night reduces exposure to daytime predators, but they still face nighttime predators. Raccoons, birds and fish will attack hatchlings, as they think of them as a tasty dinner.

Hatchlings leave the nest and head to the water in groups. Studies have shown that some nests will produce hatchlings on more than one night.

Chapter Twelve

HATCHLINGS-ON-THE-GO

C. Reaching the ocean.

 1. There are several theories as to how hatchlings find the sea.

   a. Hatchlings may discriminate light intensities and head for the greater light intensity of the open horizon. So they move towards the light.

   b. During the crawl to the sea, the hatchling may set an internal magnetic compass, which it uses for navigation away from the beach.

So if you think about it, we humans are pretty helpless in comparison to turtles. We can't find our way to our local Starbucks without Google Maps. With the exception of wilderness-loving explorers, of course.

 2. When a hatchling reaches the surf, it dives into a wave and rides the undertow out to sea, a lot like a surfer.

   a. A "swim frenzy" of continuous swimming takes place for about 24 to 48 hours after the hatchling enters the water, which is very energetic for a newborn. Human babies can only cry!

   b. This frantic activity gets the young turtle into deeper water, where it is less vulnerable to predators, who are always on the lookout for a tasty turtle snack.

   c. There have been reports of swimming hatchlings diving straight down when birds and even airplanes appear overhead. This diving behavior may be a behavioral adaptation for avoiding predation by birds.

Chapter Thirteen

A year of firsts: HATCHLINGS

D. The first year.

1. During the first few years, many species of sea turtles are rarely seen. These years are known as the "lost years."

2. Researchers generally agree that most hatchlings spend their first few years living an oceanic existence before appearing in coastal areas. Although the migratory patterns of the young turtles during the first year has long been a puzzle, most researchers believe that they ride prevailing surface currents, situating themselves in floating seaweed where they are camouflaged and where they can find food.

3. Research suggests that flatback hatchlings do not go through an oceanic phase. Evidence shows that the young turtles remain inshore following the initial swim frenzy. Most remain within 15 km (9.3 miles) of land. These little guys are the 'homebodies' of the sea turtle population.

Chapter Fourteen

ROLL CALL!

Can you remember the 8 sea turtle species? You thought I was kidding about the test earlier, right? I was kidding :-)

Green Sea Turtle

Black Sea Turtle

Leatherback Sea Turtle

Loggerhead Sea Turtle

Hawksbill Sea Turtle

Kemp's Ridley Sea Turtle

Olive Ridley Sea Turtle

Flatback Sea Turtle

Chapter Fifteen

First up: GREEN SEA TURTLES, most common turtle of 'em all

Green Sea Turtle Facts

Description

The Green Sea Turtle is a fairly large species with a length of about 5 ½ feet (can you imagine it standing up on its hind legs? It would be human sized!) and weighing up to 400 pounds (which is much more than the average linebacker). It has a hard shell on the outside that can be quite colorful on the top with shades of red and orange. It is believed that the colors of it will change throughout the course of each turtle's life, sort of like a a human dying their hair, only natural!

Distribution

You will find the Green Sea Turtle out there in the tropical and subtropical regions. Hawaii has one of the largest populations of them in the world. Other locations where they have been identified include Australia, Mexico, India, and Asia, so there are sea turtles all over the world.

Behavior

These turtles love sunbathing, after crawling up on the beach to find a good spot to soak up the sun, deep diving, as long as they can come up every four or five minutes for air, and sunbathing! (You notice a theme here, right?) So how do sea turtles drown? Well, it's very stressful to hold your breath for that long under-water, and eventually their natural mechanism stops functioning properly.

Diet /Feeding

Sea turtles, as you know, migrate thousands of miles in search of food and nesting grounds, but what you may not know is that turtles change their minds about what food they like as they get older. As new hatchlings entering the water, they

are meat eaters. When they are about 3 years of age they change to being vegetarians, so they stop eating any type of meat in the water. They consume algae
and sea grass, which isn't very filling, so they have to consume large amounts of
it every day so they don't get hungry. Imagine eating nothing but seaweed all day
long, every day, for the rest of your life!

Reproduction

As with everything else they do, sea turtles put far more effort into this than
humans. Males will return to their birthplace annually to mate with females. They
may have to travel around the world to find their mate. But sea turtles can't just
get on a plane to go see their girlfriend, they have to swim! Females are a lot less
predictable. They may have several breeding grounds, so they don't always end up
in the same place every year. It is believed that the female Green Sea Turtle only
mates every 2 to 4 years instead of annually.

The females dig nests in the sand in which to deposit their eggs. Mama can lay
from 100 to 200 very small eggs. She won't remain with her unborn babies until
they hatch a couple of months later. Instead they fight their way out of the eggs
and then go directly towards the water. These turtles are way too excited to hang
around on the beach, because as soon as they are born, they're ready to explore
the oceans! (And being eaten by predators is also on their minds, so they get
moving into the ocean quickly after hatching.)

Conservation

An adult Green Sea Turtle can live to be up to 80 years old if the conditions
are right. Sadly, they happen to be on the Endangered Species list at this time.
Although there are lots of people out there who are trying to protect green
sea turtles and their eggs, there are many more people who are ignorant of the
green sea turtle's plight, and they can do things to hurt turtles and
destroy their natural habitat. Some locations and organizations
that once killed the Green Sea Turtle have become wiser,
and now have thousands of turtles that they protect, that
tourists like you and I come to see.

Human interaction

Humans are a huge threat to the Green Sea Turtle. In some regions of the world, eating turtle meat is considered normal. Every year, a large number of innocent adult turtles are killed so that humans can enjoy their meals at restaurants. Even worse, turtle eggs are considered to be a great source of food as well. It isn't uncommon for these nesting areas to be raided of hundreds of eggs for human consumption.

Many Green Sea Turtles live in areas where fishing takes place on a large scale. Turtles often get caught in fishing nets, and most drown before they can be discovered and freed. Also, their natural habitat continues to be threatened due to humans moving into those beach areas. We humans love to build houses on the beach as well as restaurants, shops and other human-related buildings, but these structures do have an impact on sea turtles. The beach is where the turtles would like to lay their eggs but it's hard for a turtle to get a little privacy and lay her eggs when there are humans everywhere. Beaches can be fun for us humans, but for turtles, they are as essential as human hospitals when it comes to nesting.

Chapter Sixteen

LOGGERHEAD SEA TURTLE:
Yeah, sorta funny looking

Loggerhead Sea Turtle Facts

Description

The Loggerhead Sea Turtle has a head that is much bigger than any others out there. But before you make fun of it (yes, I can read your thoughts), I'd like to add that the overall body is shaped very similar to a heart, which is sweet, right? They have a shell that is red and brown on top, then yellow and brown on the bottom of it. They can be up to 250 pounds when they are full grown and close to four feet in length. So they are a lot smaller than their green turtle friends.

Distribution

You will find Loggerhead Sea Turtles in the Atlantic, Pacific, and Indian Oceans. They prefer to be in areas that offer beaches full of grainy sand. This is why you will find so many of them along the coast of Mexico and the Bahamas. However, they also make their homes in various lagoons and bays.

Diet /Feeding

You will notice that this sea turtle features very powerful jaws. So if you're a creature with a hard shell, don't assume this turtle will give up halfway through chowing down on you. Those powerful jaws make mincemeat out of shells. Literally. Loggerheads feed on a variety of foods including fish, crab, jellyfish, shrimp, mollusks, and crustaceans. They will generally dive deep to get these items from the bottom of the ocean. However, they are also known to feed in very shallow waters near the coast.

Reproduction

It may sound unbelievable, but the Loggerhead Sea Turtle isn't ready for reproduction until they are approximately

35 years old! These turtles are very late developers, and the courting (or dating) process takes place as the males and females are migrating to their breeding grounds. The females decide who they will mate with. In the world of sea turtles, its absolutely fine for the girl to ask the boy out on a date. Humans could really learn a lot from sea turtles!

The females can reproduce several times in a single mating season. They will deposit several nests of eggs that take up to two months to hatch. The young are completely on their own to survive when they hatch, and it is fascinating to see hundreds of them scrambling toward the water.

Human interaction

Since these sea turtles don't reproduce for many decades after they are born, there are concerns about their future. Many of the adults have been killed due to fishing nets and many of the young are destroyed due to their eggs being collected. In the past they have also been hunted for their meat and their shells. The fat from their bodies used to be used for making cosmetics and various types of medications. Sea turtle lipstick, anyone? People like Olivia Chantecaille now make cosmetic products that aim to save the sea turtles, not to harm them.

Conservation

The Loggerhead Sea Turtle currently has a status as a Threatened Species. It is closely being watched and efforts are in place to help the population increase. Hopefully with such early intervention they won't move any higher in the ranks towards being endangered. Many of the conservation efforts are focused on the older Loggerhead Sea Turtles as they are the ones able to reproduce at this time.

Conservation efforts continue so that the natural habitat of the Loggerhead Sea Turtle can be protected. Limits on where fishing equipment can be placed has been helpful. The amount of pollution in the water is another issue that has to be addressed to protect these sea turtles. On many beaches you will see blocked off areas with signs that say it is the Loggerhead Sea Turtle nesting area. This area will be closely monitored to ensure no one enters it. If you observe closely though you may be able to see the females depositing their eggs.

What has also been noticed is that many of the young have a hard time getting out of their eggs. Remember, sea turtle hatchlings have to break free of their eggs all by themselves! This is where experts come in and give them a hand. Since many of these young Loggerhead Sea Turtles would die without their intervention, so this helps to promote more of them having a chance of survival. They are released into the water which means they won't be prey for birds either as they make their way from the beach to the water.

Chapter Seventeen

The grandpa of sea turtles: OLD, OLD, OLD Leatherbacks

Leatherback Sea Turtle Facts

Description

The Leatherback Sea Turtle is the largest of all species that live in the water. It also ranks as the fourth largest reptile in the world. It is only beat out by three species of crocodiles. The biggest difference from other sea turtles is that it doesn't feature a hard shell. It does have layers of oily skin there instead. You will also notice that the Leatherback Sea Turtle doesn't have any teeth and has longer flippers than other sea turtles. Fully grown, these turtles can weigh as much as 2,000 pounds and grow to 8 feet long. That's the same weight as a Volkswagen Beetle.

Distribution

Leatherback Sea Turtles are found all over the world where there are oceans. They are able to dive very far so they tend to enjoy the deeper waters. Some of the most common locations including Florida, Puerto Rico, and St. Croix. They tend to live in both waters that are cold and those that are warm, so they are quite adaptable. Since they have to be able to dig nests with their flippers, they only live in the waters along sandy beaches.

Diet and Feeding

They are relentless when it comes to searching for food. It is common for them to travel hundreds of miles if they must, to find enough food to live on. Their main source of food comes from jellyfish. It's a bit like a human consuming doughnuts every day because they taste good. Eventually, those doughnuts will come back to bite you! Sea turtles' bodies have a hard time digesting the jellies, so many of them die due to an intestinal blockage. They also consume other items in the water that resemble jellyfish, including plastic bags. The kind of plastic bags you and I take home from the grocery store.

Reproduction

The mating of Leatherback sea turtles actually takes place in the water. The time of year that they will mate depends on where they reside. Mating occurs between 6 and 10 years of age. The females seem to mature years earlier than the males. (You know this is true for some humans as well, just ask your mom.) :-) There is still plenty that isn't known about the mating process for Leatherbacks, such as how they select their mates.

Young Leatherback Turtles are hatched from eggs that are often buried in the sand on land to protect them from predators. A female can lay up to 100 eggs at a time. She will nest several times in one breeding season. The egg deposits will likely be about 12 days apart. It takes between 50 and 75 days for the eggs to hatch.

Those that survive will hatch, and then instinctively move to the water. Many of them never reach the water though, due to birds feeding on them, like sea gulls. Those that do reach the water instinctively already know how to swim. They don't have any interaction with their mother, as she leaves the nest as soon as she lays her eggs.

Conservation

The Leatherback Sea Turtle doesn't have to worry too much about predators in the water. However, they need protection due to drastically low numbers. Many of them are never able to hatch due to humans and other predators getting to the eggs. Various types of pollution in the water can also cause them to become ill and die. As a result of all of this, the Leatherback Turtle is classified as an Endangered Species. It is estimated that there are approximately 115,000 of them remaining in the world.

Human Interaction

Humans continue to collect the eggs from Leatherback Turtles. In many parts of the world they are considered to be a delicacy. This has lead to a huge decline in the number of them left in the world. It is estimated that at least 1,500 of them get caught in the nets of fishermen annually as well. Those that aren't injured or killed are tossed back into the water. But some of them are already dead when they are tossed back.

Chapter Eighteen

All heart:
HAWKSBILL SEA TURTLE

Hawksbill Sea Turtle Facts

Description

The Hawksbill Sea Turtle has a heart-shaped shell on its body. As the turtle gets older that heart shape will change and the shell will get longer. Its head is small and tapered, with a mouth that resembles the beak of a bird. They have two pairs of scales along the front of their bodies.

This heart-marked turtle is smaller than most of its sea turtle friends, at less than three feet and weighing no more than 300 pounds. (The average domestic house cat weighs around 9 pounds.) They have small claws on their front flippers and are slow-moving on land.

Distribution

The majority of Hawksbill Sea Turtles live in the tropical areas of both the Atlantic and Pacific oceans. Yet there are also large numbers of them in colder areas including around Massachusetts and New Jersey, in the United States. They love to be in rocky areas and mainly stay in the shallow waters. It is unusual to find them more than 65 feet below the surface.

Generally, anywhere you find coral reef areas you will find an abundance of Hawksbill Sea Turtles. They spend most of their time in the water but they are good climbers on land in order to get to the sandy areas to deposit their eggs.

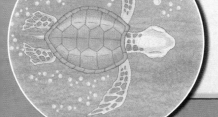

Diet /Feeding

The main source of food for the Hawkbill Sea Turtle is sponges. They are very particular about the types of them that they consume. They also eat jellyfish, fish, mollusks, crustaceans, and worms to satisfy their need for food.

Reproduction

Females are ready to mate when they are about three years of age and for males it is about four years of age. Mating only takes place every two or three years for the females. The process occurs in the shallow waters near the beaches. The female decides who she will mate with. There are some theories that the males and females mate with the same turtle each time but there isn't enough evidence at this time to confirm that.

The females will go to the beach to make a nest where she will deposit the eggs. In a single mating season she will do this about three times. Each set of eggs will be deposited about 15 days apart. She will lay from 100 to 150 eggs at a time. It will take approximately 60 days for the eggs to hatch.

The offspring are very susceptible to predators while they are young. This is due to them not being able to dive yet. Therefore they have to live at the surface of the water near the coastline. Many of them are consumed by predators, before they even make it to the water. For sea turtle hatchlings, making it to the ocean is a lot like attempting a terrifying obstacle course.

Human interaction

For centuries humans have consumed the Hawksbill Sea Turtle for its meat. They have also taken the eggs for their own consumption which prevents the population from growing. Another common problem was the selling of shells from the Hawksbill Sea Turtle. This was mainly a market in Japan that has been banned since 1993. Did you know? The Japanese people traditionally used bekko (their name for the Hawksbill's shell) to make wedding combs, that were given to a new bride.

Conservation

It is estimated that a Hawkbill Sea Turtle can live up to 50 years in the wild. Even adult Hawksbill Sea Turtles have many predators that they have to watch out for. They include raccoons, sharks, crocodiles, and large fish. The exact number of Hawksbill sea turtles that remain has proven to be difficult to accurately estimate.

Even so, it is now illegal to hunt or to kill the Hawksbill Sea Turtle in many areas of the world. It is believed that there are low enough numbers for them to be placed on the Endangered Species list. In order to find out how effective conservation efforts have been, a good count on the number of Hawksbill sea turtles that are left needs to be compiled.

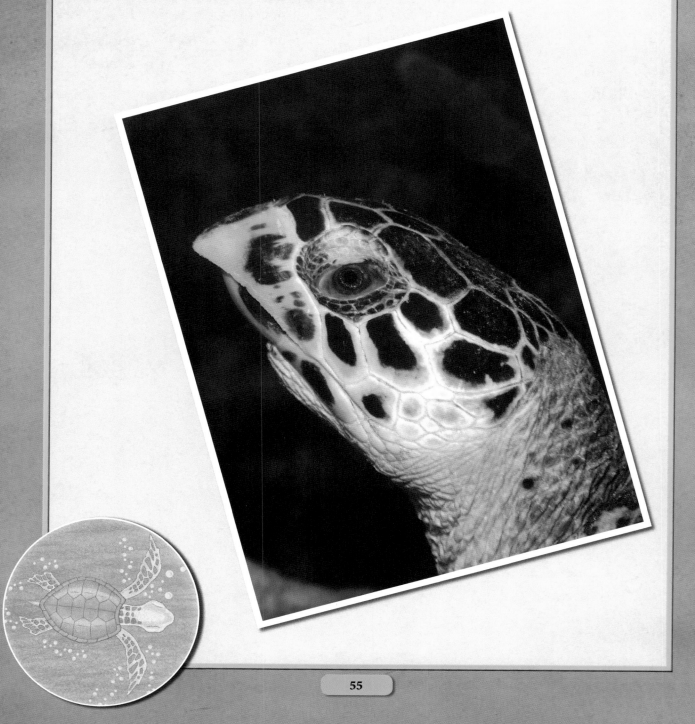

Chapter Nineteen

Small n' sweet:
OLIVE RIDLEY SEA TURTLE

Olive Ridley Sea Turtle Facts

Description

Featuring a gray and green coloring as well as a heart-shaped shell, the Olive Ridley Sea Turtle is one many people are familiar with. The young ones are mainly gray in color and as they get older they will become completely green. They are very small compared to other sea turtles; full grown they rarely weigh more than 100 pounds. They are also less than three feet in length as adults. In fact, they are categorized as the smallest species of sea turtle.

They have from six to nine pairs of costal (multiple ribs) and two pairs of front scales. Each of their front flippers has a set of claws that they use for digging when they reach land. The males and the females look very similar in color and size. The way you can tell them apart is that the males have a tail that sticks out and the females don't.

Distribution

The vast majority of Olive Ridley Sea Turtles can be found in the Pacific Ocean. More specifically, towards the beach areas of Mexico. They are known to be distributed in locations all over the world though. Many of them reside along the coastal regions of South America and West Africa. Other prime locations for seeing them include Southern California and Northern Chile.

They are often seen in other locations between such points. This is because they migrate hundreds of miles in search of food and to reach their breeding grounds each year.

Diet /Feeding

These sea turtles feed on shrimp, crab, lobster, and jellyfish. When these items are hard to find they will turn to consuming various types of algae that are available.

Reproduction

Maturity is approximately 15 years of age for the Olive Ridley Sea Turtle. The females will reproduce at least once a year and most of them do so at least twice. They will lay up to 100 eggs at a time. It takes approximately 50 to 60 days for them to hatch. Then they will make their journey to the water. The nesting habits of the Olive Ridley Sea Turtle are very unique when compared to other types of sea turtles out there. Instead of each female creating their own nest, they work together to create a very large one for all of them to deposit their eggs in. However, there are still some of this species that nest on their own and don't join the larger group effort.

Conservation

There aren't many conservation efforts in place right now for the Olive Ridley Sea Turtle. Approximately 800,000 of them are found in the world so one might assume that they don't need our help. However, they are classified as an Endangered Species due to the fact that their natural habitat continues to be destroyed at an alarming rate.

The fact that the number of Olive Ridley Sea Turtles has dropped more than 50% in the last 45 years is something to be concerned about. If that trend continues then they may be extinct over the next 50 years. With the right conditions for the Olive Ridley Sea Turtle, one can easily live to be at least 50 years old.

Human Interaction

In spite of conservation efforts to protect their natural habitat, they continue to be killed for their meat. They are also killed for their skin as it has many uses. The eggs of the Olive Ridley Sea Turtle often get taken by people to consume as well. In many locations they end up in fishing nets that are meant to capture other types of aquatic life. Yet many of them suffer injuries or die while in those nets.

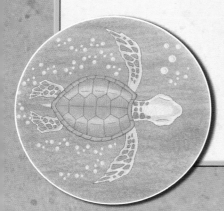

Chapter Twenty

Tiny with spots:
KEMP'S RIDLEY SEA TURTLE

Kemp's Ridley Sea Turtle Facts

Description

The Kemp's Ridley Sea Turtle is one of the smallest out there in the world. They weigh only about 100 pounds and they range in size from 2 ½ feet long to 3 feet long. They are gray and green in color with some yellow underneath their shell. They feature five pairs of costal as well as flippers that have claws on them. They are often mistaken for the Olive Ridley Sea Turtle. The main difference is the coloring of their underbelly.

They have a much darker shade of head, which is interesting as it does tend to stand out when you compare it to the lighter coloring of the rest of their bodies. They also feature spots on their heads.

Distribution

The Gulf of Mexico is the most common region where they reside. They are also plentiful around Florida, and many are found along the Mediterranean Sea. They tend to favor regions where there is plenty of algae. They use them to easily float around in the water, just like you or I would float in the pool on a hot summer's day.

Diet /Feeding

The Kemp's Ridley Sea Turtle primarily will be noticed in the water where it is muddy or sandy. This is where they find most of the prey that they usually feed upon. Their diet includes jellyfish, mollusks, and a variety of small fish. They are able to hunt for food in areas of very cold water. This is due to a mechanism that allows them to reduce their metabolism. This also allows them to remain under water for hours at a time.

Due to the way they can control their bodies' metabolism, the Kemp's Ridley Sea Turtle can be without food for a period of up to three months when necessary. I'm sure they become very hungry though!

Reproduction

Reproduction takes place in the water. The age of maturity is from 10 to 15 years for these sea turtles. They can live to be up to 50 years of age and they will annually have a deposit of eggs from the time they reach maturity.

You may find it interesting to learn that the males never come out of the water after they first find it as a new hatchling. The females only come ashore when it is time for them to deposit their eggs. Another fun fact is that females will only lay their eggs during the sunlight hours. They nest in the same beach area year after year. They may travel hundreds or even thousands of miles to reach that destination.

The females engage in a synchronized deposit of their eggs (so their motions are timed, like you or I when we dance to a choreographed routine) on land into a nesting area that they dig. This is very unique behavior and one that the Olive Ridley Sea Turtles also take part in. One of these huge nesting grounds is in Rancho Nuevo, Mexico. Many tourists come to this location to observe the behaviors of the female Kemp's Ridley Sea Turtles.

Nesting takes place from May through July depending on the location. Each female will lay approximately 100 eggs that will hatch about 60 days later.

Conservation

Based on some slow increases in their numbers, it is believed that conservation efforts for the Kemp's Ridley Sea Turtle have been helpful. However, they continue to lose their natural habitat as more of the beaches are used for people and other developments. They also face problems in the water due to pollution and predators. At this point in time they are considered to be the most endangered type of sea turtle in the world.

Human interaction

It is believed approximately 60% of all the eggs nested by the Kemp's Ridley Sea Turtles are taken by local villagers as a source of food.

Chapter Twenty-One

Aussie time:
FLATBACK SEA TURTLE

Common Name: Australian flatback—named because its shell is very flat.

Scientific Name: *Natator depressus*

Description: Their heads have a single pair of prefrontal scales (scales in front of their eyes). The carapace is bony without ridges and has large, non-overlapping, scutes (scales) present with only 4 lateral scutes. The carapace is oval or round and the body is very flat. The flippers have 1 single claw. The edge of the carapace is folded and covered by thin, non-overlapping waxy scutes. The carapace is also olive-grey with pale brown and yellow tones on its margins and the flippers are a creamy white. The scutes of the hatchlings form a unique dark-grey reticulate pattern, and the center of each scute is olive colored.

Size: Adults measure up to 3.25 feet in carapace length (99 cm).

Weight: Adults weigh an average of 198 pounds (90 kg).

Diet: Apparently eats sea cucumbers, jellyfish, mollusks, prawns, bryozoans, other invertebrates and seaweed.

Habitat: Prefer turbid inshore waters, bays, coastal coral reef and grassy shallows.

Nesting: Nests 4 times per season. Lays an average of 50 eggs at time, but these are comparatively quite large. The eggs incubate for about 55 days. When the hatchlings emerge, they are larger than most species.

Range: Very limited. It is found only in the waters around Australia and Papua New Guinea in the Pacific.

Status: *Australia*—Listed as Vulnerable under the Australian Environment Protection & Biodiversity Conservation Act. *International*—Listed as Data Deficient by the International Union for Conservation of Nature and Natural Resources. Was previously listed as vulnerable. The change in classification does not imply species recovery, it just indicates a lack of recent research into their abundance and distribution.

Threats to Survival: Sea turtles are threatened with capture, harvesting of eggs, destruction of nesting beaches, ocean pollution, oil spills and entanglement in fishing and shrimp nets.

Population Estimate*: 20,285 nesting females.

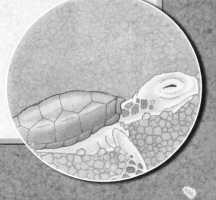

Chapter Twenty-Two

SAVING SEA TURTLES:
Pollution

The oceans may be vast, but they aren't vast enough to cope with the amount of pollution created in our cities, towns and farms. Pollution can kill or harm sea turtles. Everyday things we use, such as oil in our cars, or fertilizers on our lawns, contributes to urban runoff that travels from drains and rivers in our towns, directly into the ocean. Sewage and oil often enters the food chain. Oil spills also contribute to the loss of sea turtle nesting and feeding grounds. Also, sea turtles can become entangled in waste, causing them to drown.

Did you know? Turtles often mistake plastic bags for jellyfish! While this might sound like an amusing mistake, plastic bags (which don't biodegrade, so they stay around forever) can get stuck in a sea turtle's intestines, causing a blockage which kills them. Sea turtles can even get stuck in plastic 6-pack holders, and suffer from deformed shells because they can't grow properly. Imagine having a 6-pack holder stuck around your arm for the rest of your life - it would be very uncomfortable, right?

In recent years, the smart folk who study marine life have noticed a worrying increase in fibropapillomas. These are very unpleasant tumors that appear all over a sea turtle's skin, eyes, mouth and even their internal organs. Unfortunately, the fibropapilloma virus is now an epidemic among green sea turtles, and turtles suffer from it in the same way that humans suffer from cancer. Water pollution is considered to be a likely cause of the virus, which is helping to drive our sea turtle friends to extinction.

So what can we do? We can minimize the amount of waste that finds its way into the ocean by recycling. Packing materials like styrofoam are deadly to sea turtles. Instead of taking your groceries home in plastic bags, why not buy a reusable shopping bag? Or recycle any plastic bottles, bags or any other form of plastic you use.

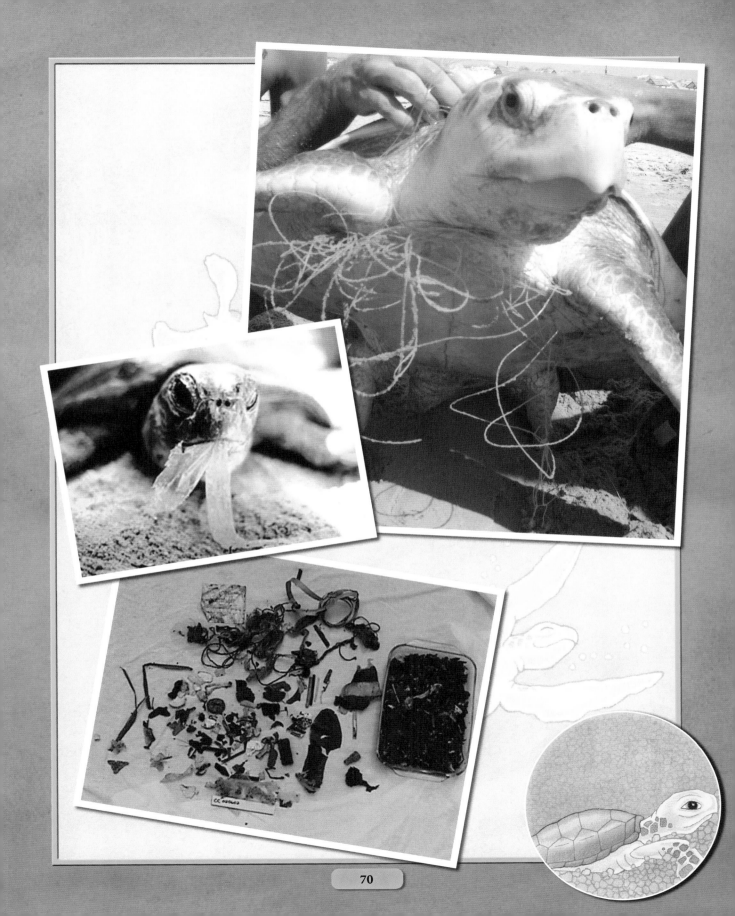

Chapter Twenty-Three

SAVING SEA TURTLES:
Oil Spills

Have you ever seen a sea turtle covered in oil? I hope not, because if you have, I'm sure you were very sad, and quite indignant. Sea turtles don't like being covered in oil, just as you or I would hate being soaked in such foul-smelling liquid. Oil spills caused by accidents at large oil rigs or wells can cause tremendous stress and danger for sea turtles. When a sea turtle is covered in oil, they are very likely to die. This is because oil contains toxic chemicals, that can damage a sea turtle's vital organs. Injuries, deformities, respiratory problems, gastrointestinal tract and brain damage, are common symptoms found in turtles who are victims of oil spills.

Mama sea turtles may not be able to have as many hatchlings, resulting in even less turtles being born. The sea turtle population is already so small, that fewer hatchlings and deaths from oil spills may mean the extinction of one or more species. Sea turtles can't avoid the oil, because often their breeding grounds, or foraging grounds are affected, making it hard for them to nest—and eat! So what can we do about it? Well, some people save sea turtles and hatchlings that are victims of terrible oil spills, such as the Gulf oil spill, by caring for injured sea turtles, and rescuing them from polluted waters and beaches, but until human beings can stop being so reliant on oil for our cars and manufacturing, more sea turtles will continue to die in oil spill disasters.

Chapter Twenty-Four

SAVING SEA TURTLES:
Global Warming

Global warming may mean that your favorite beach disappears, which would be sad for you, because it's a place you know and love, but imagine how a sea turtle would feel about their beach disappearing. Remember how we talked about sea turtles returning to the same beaches to nest for their whole lives? Well, global warming could mean rising tides, disappearing

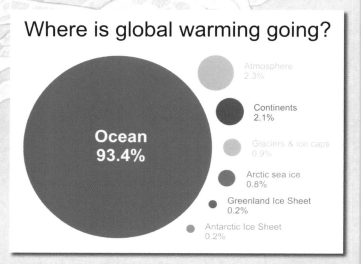

Where is global warming going?

Ocean 93.4%

Atmosphere 2.3%

Continents 2.1%

Glaciers & ice caps 0.9%

Arctic sea ice 0.8%

Greenland Ice Sheet 0.2%

Antarctic Ice Sheet 0.2%

nesting grounds, and rising temperatures. Sea turtle nesting grounds have been established for thousands of years, so how quickly could a sea turtle adapt? Not quick enough. It may take ten thousand years for new sea turtle breeding grounds to be reestablished.[1] So where would they go to nest? And how would hatchlings cope with rising tides? And what would they eat (and where) if their food sources vanish?

Unfortunately, since the gender of a hatchling is determined by the temperature of the eggs, male sea turtles could stop being born if temperatures rise! That would mean the extinction of the species.

The easiest way to save sea turtles from global warming is to think about all the ways in which we can conserve energy in our homes, by turning off lights, using less water, and limiting our use of fossil fuels. This may sound really hard and boring, but the sea turtles will thank you every time you remember to turn off your bathroom light.

1 The Sea Turtle Restoration Project. http://seaturtles.org/article.php?id=988 Accessed: 11/9/12. 17:26

Chapter Twenty-Five

SAVING SEA TURTLES:
Hunting

Humans are the biggest predators of sea turtles. Our species have found ways to use and sell almost every part of a sea turtle's body, from their shell down to their body fat, so every year thousands of sea turtles are hunted, despite international efforts to save them from extinction. Humans eat sea turtle meat and eggs, which are considered

GREEN TURTLE ON WHARF AT KEY WEST

delicacies in some countries. We use their body fat for oil, we make their shells into jewelry and tourist souvenirs, and we use their skin to make leather goods, like purses. In China, turtle eggs are used in traditional medicine. In some parts of the world, hatchlings are killed and stuffed, then sold as curios.

Commercial fishing is the biggest threat to turtles. Sea turtles get caught in fishing nets intended for tuna shrimp, or other fish, then drown because they cannot reach the surface to breath.

Hunting sea turtles isn't just cruel; it's also unsustainable. Sea turtles reproduce and develop slowly, just like humans. But unlike humans, sea turtles are nearly extinct.

Chapter Twenty-Six

SAVING SEA TURTLES:
Big Business

Trading sea turtles for commercial gain is banned under the 'Convention on International Trade in Endangered Species' (known as CITES), but illegal commercial trading of turtles is still common, particularly in Japan, where the rare hawksbill turtle (known in Japan as bekko) is coveted for its beautiful shell. Jewelry, ornaments, combs, and sunglasses are made from marine turtle shells in Asia, and in China, parts of turtles are still used to make traditional medicines. Turtles are also sold as exotic pets internationally, disrupting turtle mating and breeding rituals.

Many commercial fishermen don't want to use turtle-friendly nets or Turtle Exclusion Devices (or TED's), which allow sea turtles a means of escape. They are more difficult to use, and many fishermen prefer using gill nets, which kill and maim sea turtles. Fishermen are afraid that new fishing techniques will mean less profit, and destroy their livelihood and fishing heritage. But what about the sea turtle's heritage? Sea turtles have been around millions of years longer than humans, and their nesting and feeding grounds are thousands of years old. Fishermen can use TED's and turtle-friendly nets without significantly affecting their catches, which trials of TED's have proven, but they are not using them on a wide scale. Humans are on a path to destroy this beautiful marine animal for profit. Unfortunately, sea turtles won't be the first creature to become extinct because we over-hunted them.

Big oil companies which dredge for oil along the coast or offshore are a threat to sea turtle mating and nesting. Lobbyists for oil companies frequently try to make amendments to legislation, like the ESA, which protects sea turtles. You can help by being aware of legislation that seeks to put company profits above the lives of marine turtles, and by writing letters to your local politicians, encouraging them to stop big oil companies from expanding and operating offshore, where sea turtles like to play, eat and mate.

Chapter Twenty-Seven

ANGELS AMONG US:
Sea Turtle Rescues

Luckily for sea turtles, there are some very caring people out there who rescue and revive sea turtles who are sick or injured. Rescue centers like 'The Karen Beasley Sea Turtle Rescue And Rehabilitation Center' (quite a mouthful!) or the international organization 'Sea Turtle Rescue' venture out into the water and save the lives of sea turtles injured by boat propellors, fishing lines, and other debris we leave laying around in the ocean and on beaches. These angels also patrol the beaches at night to check that nesting turtles are healthy, untangling poor sea turtles from nets and ensuring turtles receive medical treatment when necessary. These saviors of sea turtles don't get paid (they volunteer—you can too!) and they do it all out of the goodness of their hearts (and their love of sea turtles, of course).

Rescue centers, hospitals and other sea turtle organizations need money, human volunteers, and donations of items that you may have laying around the house, like backpacks, surfboards, kayaks, GPS unit or weighing scales. You can donate stuff by going to their websites. Check with your parents before you donate any items, or you might get the sea turtles (and you) in trouble!

Chapter Twenty-Eight

ANGELS AMONG US:
Sea Turtle Hospitals

After sea turtles are rescued, they normally receive medical treatment before they can return to the wild. Sea turtle hospitals have a very hot, dirty and smelly job. They have to feed and do laundry for each turtle, as well as administer to their wounds, give them medicine, perform surgery, and clean and refill sea turtle tanks.

Sea turtles have very different personalities, just like humans, so each turtle needs different care. Some sea turtles are picky eaters, others have severe injuries, and some are just cranky, like your Grandpa Joe. Sea turtles that end up in these hospitals are often gravely injured, and may need a flipper amputated, or have carapace fractures. They may have deformities, be weak, or be suffering from malnutrition. The angels who work at these hospitals pamper their sea turtles, making them feel at home. Each turtle is named by their rescuers—if you don't believe me, check out some of their amazing names! The rescued turtles come in all types, shapes and sizes. If you want to help, you can adopt a sea turtle, and help care for it while it is staying in hospital. You can receive a photo of your adopted turtle, as well as email updates!

Some turtle hospitals include **The Turtle Hospital:** www.turtlehospital.org/blog/ in Florida, the hospital at the **South Carolina Aquarium:** www.scaquarium.org/str/hospital/default.aspx, the **Mote Marine Laboratory, Florida:** www.mote.org/index.php?src=gendocs&ref=Sea%20Turtle%20Rehabilitation%20Hospital&category=Animal%20Care%20Programs, and the Georgia Sea **Turtle Center:** www.georgiaseaturtlecenter.org/.

Take a look at the hospital websites to see all the cute sea turtles! There are baby turtles, grown-up turtles and turtles who could be professional sumo-wrestlers (if they weren't turtles).

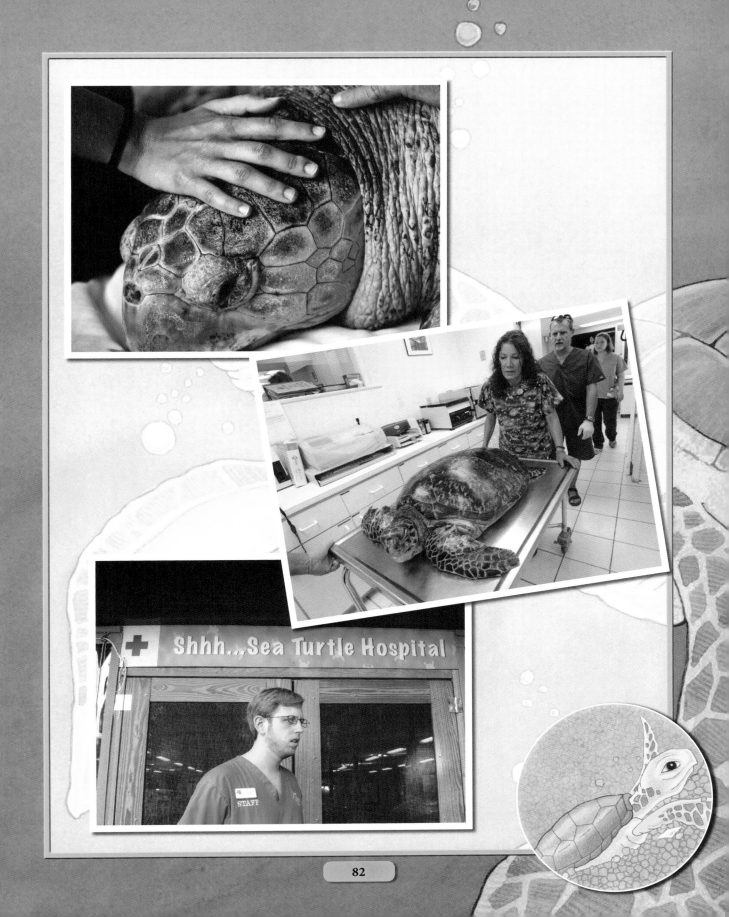

Shhh...Sea Turtle Hospital

Chapter Twenty-Nine

ANGELS AMONG US:
Sea Turtle Releases

So what happens once sea turtles recover? They are released back into the ocean, of course! For some people who adopt turtles, watching their turtle friend being released back into the ocean to start their new life can be both a happy and sad event. It's always wonderful to witness a sea turtle recovery, but hard to say goodbye, especially knowing the scary, polluted state of our oceans.

Most organizations hold sea turtle release days. On these days, you can go to the beach and watch lots of fully recovered, healthy turtles being sent back to their home—the sea! Huge crowds normally gather to wave the sea turtles off, and to wish them good luck in their new life. Sea turtles who leave their temporary hospital home can be tracked using transmitters in the ocean, to see where they travel, how long they live after release, and more.

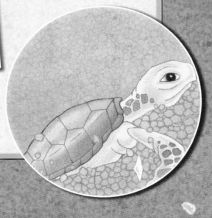

Chapter Thirty

ANGELS AMONG US:
Sea Turtle Organizations

One of the most important missions that sea turtle organizations carry out is to protect hatchlings. They do this through their nightly beach patrols, looking for turtle tracks in the sand (they look a bit like tractor tire markings) tracking down nests, and on rare occasions, moving nests if they are in danger from the tide, or in an unsuitable location, to give the hatchlings the best chance of survival.

The Turtle Foundation works all over the world rescuing sea turtles, in exotic places like Berau, Indonesia, and Boavista, Cape Verde. Unfortunately, poaching is common in these areas, and the Sea Turtle Foundation has its work cut out to protect Loggerhead turtles from being harvested for their meat during nesting. The organization monitors nesting turtles in an effort to prevent females from being killed. You can become a member of the Sea Turtle Foundation or adopt a sea turtle on their website: www.turtle-foundation.org

The Sea Turtle Restoration Project in California holds events abroad, where volunteers can tag sea turtles, as well as protecting and raising awareness of the sea turtles' plight in the Pacific Rim. The organization campaigns for turtle-friendly legislation and promotes important issues such as the 'Save the Leatherback' campaign. www.seaturtles.org/

Most sea turtle organizations in the U.S. are located where the turtles are at, so that means they are generally found in Florida and along the East Coast. You can find out about all the sea turtle groups at www.seaturtle.org, which has a map showing which organization is nearest your location. There are several in Florida, but they include the Boca Raton Sea Turtle Program, at the Gumbo Limbo Nature Center. They hold a sea turtle day festival every year around March, and have many other fun events and programs for the public. At Boca Raton, they research and care for sea turtles, releasing healthy turtles back into the wild. www.gumbolimbo.org/ The Bald Head Island Conservancy (BHIC) has to be mentioned because of its fun turtle tours! If you're lucky enough to be in North Carolina, check out their website. They count the number of turtles they spot on the islands every year, including how many nests are laid and hatched! They hold events like 'Turtle Trot' and 'Touch Tank Time' every week.

GREEN SEA TURTLE
(Chelonia mydas)

The Green Sea Turtle is a common sea turtle found in the waters of the Gulf of Mexico. This turtle received its name from the color of its body fat, which is green from the algae it consumes. The Green Sea Turtle was added to the endangered/threatened species list on July 28, 1978. Its smooth carapace with coloration that can be gray, green, brown, and black can identify this turtle. Its plastron is usually colored yellowish-white. Adult Green Sea Turtles usually weigh between 200 - 400 pounds and have distribution worldwide in tropical and subtropical waters. The diet of a Green Sea Turtle changes dramatically throughout its life. Juveniles usually are omnivores, eating anything from fish to algae. Adults are usually herbivores and consume algae and sea grass. Nesting occurs from March until October in the Gulf of Mexico, with the greatest activity from June until August. In Florida, the wild Green Sea Turtle population can lay anywhere from 200 - 1100 nests a year on statewide beaches. Females can lay on average 75 - 200 eggs in one clutch, with an average clutch size of 135 eggs in Florida and an incubation period of 48 - 70 days.

Chapter Thirty-One

Naw really! SEA TURTLE EDUCATION FOR KIDS

By now, you're probably getting sick of my suggestions to adopt a sea turtle, but just in case you're not, please, please adopt a sea turtle! Nearly every sea turtle organization allows you to adopt a sea turtle for your very own, so click on the links above to donate and see a picture of

your new friend. The Sea Turtle Foundation is a great place to start, as well as the Karen Beasley Foundation, because they have a wonderful patient index, showing the names, pictures, and current status of your turtle friends.

And now for the fun stuff ! Sea turtles may have it rough, but it's not all doom and gloom. A fantastic way to raise awareness about sea turtles and their problems is to make turtle-related crafts, like sea turtles cupcakes, sea turtle scarfs, sea turtle pottery . . . the possibilities are endless. Whether you sell these wonderful creations, and donate the proceeds to sea turtle charities, or give your handmade sea turtle crafts to friends and family as gifts, you'll be helping to spread the word about marine turtles.

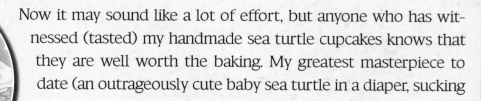

Now it may sound like a lot of effort, but anyone who has witnessed (tasted) my handmade sea turtle cupcakes knows that they are well worth the baking. My greatest masterpiece to date (an outrageously cute baby sea turtle in a diaper, sucking on a dummy) was widely regarded (possibly) as the greatest sea turtle cupcake ever made, in the history of the world of baby sea turtle cupcakes, of which I'm sure there are many, many turtle cupcakes. :-) Sea turtles also work well as birthday cakes, because of their big round shell and cute faces. (Not real sea turtles, obviously, since they really don't like it when you try to stick candles into their shells.)

For talented knitters, crocheters, and sewers (people who sew clothes, not the smelly place where wastewater goes), cute sea turtle scarfs or hats are really easy to make. Paper mache or clay sea turtles are great for classroom projects. If you want a cool and relaxing bathroom decoration, you can glue stones together in the shape of a sea turtle.

Chapter Thirty-Two

THOSE IN CELESTIAL ORBIT ABOVE THE REST

SEA TURTLE PIONEERS, SCIENTISTS, ACTIVISTS

Despite not knowing many politicians who can speak on their behalf, sea turtles do have some friends in high places. The kind of rare friends that stand up to bullies, or in this case, to the slow extermination of the entire marine turtle species. These friends are scientists, activists, and pioneers in their fields of research.

A very famous friend to the sea turtles was Archie Carr. Carr studied Zoology (the biology of animals) and was in fact a herpetologist (he loved amphibians). The amphibians he loved best of all were marine turtles, and he did all he could to show people what the loss of their habitat would mean for sea turtles. He founded Tortuguera (it means Land of Turtles) National Park, in Costa Rica in 1975. Tortuguera's beaches attract many endangered turtles, and so Carr established a safe place for the sea turtles to nest. Carr lived from 1909–1987, but his work lives on, and his efforts are sustained through the Caribbean Conservation Corporation, and the many books he wrote, including 'The Windward Road', and 'So Excellent A Fishe: A Natural History of Sea Turtles'. Did you know? World Sea Turtle Day, on June 16th, was chosen because it coincides with Dr. Carr's birthday. At one time, Carr was considered to be the person who knew most about sea turtles in the entire world!

Chapter Thirty-Three

BOOKS, LEGENDS, LORE:
Sea Turtles In Literature

Sea turtles are everywhere—and I don't just mean in the oceans and on our beaches. Sea turtles have been popular movie stars, fictional characters in books, and they are even worshipped!

Top 10 children's books about sea turtles:

1. I'll Follow the Moon by Stephanie Lisa Tara (of course it's number one!)

2. Turtle Bay by Saviour Pirotta and Nilesh Mistry.

3. The Voyage of Turtle Rex by Kurt Cyrus.

4. Limu the Blue Turtle and His Hawaiian Garden by Kimo Armitage and Scott Kaneshiro.

5. Turtle Splash! Countdown at the Pond by Cathryn Falwell.

6. Mamma Sea Turtle Lost Her Babies by Robert Stanek.

7. Dash the Sea Turtle by Kim Costello, Frank Costello and Sean Kilgore.

8. Tammy Turtle: A Tale of Saving Sea Turtles by Suzanne Tate and James Melvin.

9. Squishy Turtle and Friends (Cloth Books) by Roger Priddy.

10. Baby Turtle's Tale by Elle J. Mcguinness and Romi Caron.

Top 10 Kid's Scientific / Non-Fiction Books:

1. National Geographic Readers: Sea Turtles by Laura Marsh

2. Sea Turtles: Amazing Photos & Fun Facts on Animals in Nature (Our Amazing World Series) by Kay de Silva.

3. Owen & Mzee: The True Story of a Remarkable Friendship by Isabella Hatkoff, Craig Hatkoff, Paula Kahumbu, and Peter Greste.

4. The Life Cycle of a Sea Turtle (Nature's Life Cycles) by Anna Kingston.

5. Sea Turtles (Undersea Encounters) by Mary Jo Rhodes and David Hall.

6. Into the Sea by Brenda Z. Guiberson and Alix Berenzy.

7. Sea Turtle Journey—a Smithsonian Oceanic Collection Book by Lorraine A. Jay and Katie Lee.

8. Endangered Sea Turtles (Earth's Endangered Animals) by Bobbie Kalman.

9. Leatherback Sea Turtle (Animals in Danger) by Rod Theodorou.

10. Interrupted Journey: Saving Endangered Sea Turtles by Kathryn Lasky.

Adult Books about Sea Turtles:

1. Sea Turtles: An Ecological Guide by David Gulko and Karen Eckert.

2. Saving Sea Turtles: Extraordinary Stories from the Battle against Extinction by James R. Spotila.

3. Sea Turtles of the Atlantic And Gulf Coasts of the United States (A Wormsloe Foundation Nature Book) by Carol Ruckdeschel and C. Robert Shoop.

4. Voyage of the Turtle: In Pursuit of the Earth's Last Dinosaur by Carl Safina.

5. The Windward Road: Adventures of a Naturalist on Remote Caribbean Shores by Archie F. Carr.

6. So Excellent a Fishe: A Natural History of Sea Turtles by Archie F. Carr.

7. The Biology of Sea Turtles volumes 1 and 2 by Peter Lutz.

8. Loggerhead Sea Turtles by Alan B. Bolten and Blair E. Witherington.

9. Fire In The Turtle House: The Green Sea Turtle and the Fate of the Ocean by Osha Gray Davidson.

10. Biology and Conservation of Ridley Sea Turtles by Pamela T. Plotkin.

Don't just read about sea turtles, watch them as they journey through the oceans! There are lots of DVD's featuring turtles including the fun: 'A Turtle's Tale: Sammy's Adventures' or the more serious: 'Turtle: The Incredible Journey'.

Artists love sea turtles too. Beautiful sea turtle photographs or cute cartoon art make stunning decor, and can be used as a conversation piece (where you can tell your friends all about the plight of sea turtles).

In world culture, sea turtles play an important part in creation myths and legends, especially in stories passed down by almost all of the Native American tribes. The 'Earth Diver' myth tells the story of how North America was created when a turtle dived to the bottom of the ocean, and retrieved a lump of mud, which became the continent we know as America. Some Native Americans still call this land 'Turtle Island'. The turtle supposedly supports the earth on its back, so Native Americans still hold the sea turtle in high regard. Luckily North America isn't really supported on the back of a turtle, and we are not all in danger of drowning when the sea turtle decides to dive again.

In Hawaii, the green sea turtle symbolizes wisdom (because of the sea turtle's longevity), peace, and good luck. The sea turtle is native to the islands, and in legend, the 'honu' as the sea turtle is known, is famous for giving protection to those in need. The guardian spirits Kailua and Honu-po'o-kea (daughter and mother) are central figures in Hawaiian mythology, and gave the Hawaiians fresh spring water as a gift. At Pu'u Loa lava fields, in Hawaii Volcanoes National Park, there is a sea turtle petroglyph (a drawing etched into rock). The petroglyphs trail is sacred to Hawaiians and has over 23,000 petroglyphs. The sea turtle at Pu'u Loa is depicted swimming, and shows just how much the ancient people respected this amphibious navigator.

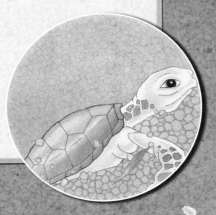

EPILOGUE

Sea turtles are incredible creatures. They survived when the dinosaurs perished. They travel thousands of miles to their nesting grounds, they never forget where they were born, and they are amazing navigators. Sea turtles mature and reproduce slowly, and need access to beaches (which are their ancient nesting grounds) and a food supply. Human thirst for oil, environmental disasters, boat propellors, artificial lighting, and the growing human population invading turtle territories, is killing sea turtles at a faster rate than they can reproduce.

These magnificent creatures need your help. They need advocates who can speak up for them, they need politicians of the future who care about their fellow creatures more than making a quick buck, and they need ordinary people who are prepared to think before they toss a plastic bottle in the trash, drive a high-speed boat near the shoreline, or leave the lights on at night.

Human beings may have conquered the planet. But turtles were here first. Respecting their right to travel to, and nest on their beaches, to eat in their waters, without fear of human interference, just makes us better humans, right? At least I think so.

Most people are ignorant about the plight of the turtles, or don't know what they can do to stop the crimes against them. Time is running out. Spread the word. Save the sea turtles. Whether you raise awareness by giving your brother a turtle knit hat for Christmas, blog about sea turtles, or join a sea turtle organization, every action you carry out can help save the sea turtle from extinction.

HOW CAN I HELP?

S o you know you want to help save the sea turtles, but you don't know what to do? Here's an easy and fun list to help you begin your new turtle-friendly lifestyle!

How to live 'The Turtle-Friendly Lifestyle!'

1. Recycle! Most single-use packaging (like fast food containers) and plastic bottles / bags can be recycled. Sea turtles don't like eating plastic any more than you do.

2. Reuse. Reusing any packaging you receive in the mail, including packing peanuts stops these anti-sea turtle weapons from being dumped into our oceans.

3. Buy a multi-use grocery bag from your favorite store and take it on shopping trips.

4. Adopt a sea turtle! Most sea turtle organizations have an adoption option. Ask your parents to gift you a sea turtle for Christmas. You'll get photos and email updates from your new friend. Well, from the people caring for him anyway. Turtles can't use email (yet!).

5. Talk to your friends about sea turtles. Okay, I realize sea turtles may not be the coolest thing to talk about at the lunch table, but a true friend will listen to anything you say, even if you bore the pants off them with your obsession about flippers. Who knows? Maybe they'll fall in love with sea turtles too.

6. Wear sea turtle paraphernalia. T-shirts, backpacks,

hats, sea turtle costumes . . . . you get the picture. Complete strangers will see you and think of sea turtles. How cool is that? Just don't get too disappointed if your crush is too busy thinking about your sea turtle garb to think about you.

7. Walk to school (if you can, when it's safe to do so). Human beings are so reliant on oil that we hurt sea turtles. Convince your mom / dad to ditch the car and walk to the grocery store.

8. Eat environmentally-friendly tuna. By-catches of other species are common when mainstream 'dolphin-friendly' tuna is caught. Turtles and other ocean dwellers are at risk from tuna fishing and dolphin-friendly tuna labels are misleading. Check out some environmentally-friendly tuna brands recommended by the Monterey Bay Aquarium, including Pelican's Choice and Wild Planet.

9. Study politics, the environment and the law. Yeah, this is a really boring one. BUT, we need more politicians, environmental activists and animal rights lawyers in this world who care.

10. Turn out the lights. Artificial lighting confuses turtles and hatchlings, and wastes resources. Remember to turn out the lights when you leave a room, or when you go to sleep. Always put your own safety first.

11. Share the beach! Beaches are fun places to be, but remember, they are actually nesting grounds for our sea turtle friends. Don't disturb eggs or raid nests, and limit your time at the beach when possible.

12. Don't litter in our oceans or leave trash on the beach. Littering is a really gross habit anyway, so don't become a litterbug, toss your empties into a trash can or preferably, recycle! Remember, sea turtles die when they ingest plastic or other trash. Any trash left on the beach gets swept into the ocean when the tide changes.

13. Volunteer! There are loads of opportunities to help out sea turtle organizations. If there isn't one in your area, start your own Sea Turtle Appreciation Society.

14. Tweet about sea turtles. Spread the word online through social media and raise awareness.

15. Conquer the world and eliminate all opposition to sea turtles!!! (I'm kidding. Tyrannical dictatorships aren't known for their sea turtle activism.) But you can make a difference by being a good friend to sea turtles, no matter who or what you choose to be.

As a wise friend once told me: 'Live however you want, but not at anyone else's expense.' (And that includes at the expense of sea turtles.)

GLOSSARY

The Green Turtle Glossary

Congratulations! You're still reading! In fact, you have reached the very end of this unique book filled with smart and witty comments about sea turtles (probably). If you aren't still reading this, hopefully it's because you've joined a sea turtle organization, and are too busy playing with sea turtles to read.

If you still can't remember what a 'carapace' is or why you should care, this helpful glossary will answer all your sea-turtle-related questions. For answers to all other questions, please read a different book.

FACT: Memorizing this glossary will make you smarter than most of the people you know.

RECOMMENDATION: Keep this fact to yourself.

Anthropogenic—when humans interfere in nature, we make an impact on (cause change for) sea turtles.

Arribada—this is a fun Spanish word that means 'huge nest' of many sea turtles.

Basking—humans bask in the sun, just like sea turtles. We call it 'sunbathing'. Turtles like to bask for fun, and warmth, just like you and I!

Biodiversity—diversity means 'different things' and biodiversity means 'different things in nature'. The more differences there are, the better the ecosystem functions. So less types of sea turtles—a less healthy ecosystem.

Black Turtle (Chelonia mydas agassizi)—Threatened by overfishing and poaching, this black or grayshelled turtle is a rare sight to behold. It uniquely enjoys nesting in the Galapagos Islands.

Bycatch—the unintentional catching of species when fishing for a particular type of fish. Turtles are often caught in fishing nets intended for shrimp.

Carapace—this is the turtle's shell. It protects the sea turtle's body from harm.

Carnivore—meat-eating creatures (humans are primarily carnivores).

Caruncle—hatchlings have a single tooth that allows them to break free of their shell. Also see Emergence.

Cheloniid—a type or species of sea turtle that can be identified by its hard shell. This includes all sea turtles except the leatherback. See: Dermochelyid.

CITES—The Convention on International Trade in Endangered Species of Wild Fauna and Flora.

Clutch—this is what sea turtle experts call a 'group' or nest of eggs.

Conservation—protecting the environment from harm through careful management.

Dermochelyid—sea turtles species that has a leathery shell. The only member of this species that is still alive is the Leatherback Turtle.

Disorientation—sea turtles find their way by following the moon's natural lighting. So when we turn on our man-made lights, the poor sea turtles get confused, and often fail to walk in the right direction.

Diurnal—some animals are most active during the day. This is the opposite of mainly being active at night (nocturnal).

Dredging—Big machines suck up and dig out the earth that lies underwater for mining, or to improve man-made structures (like harbors). Unfortunately, sea turtles can be injured by these machines, especially if dredging takes place during the nesting season.

Ectothermic—Sea turtles are affected by their surroundings more than humans are. Their body temperature depends on the temperature of their environment.

Egg Chamber—Sea turtles make a small fortress or 'chamber' for their eggs which keeps the eggs warm and helps them develop into hatchlings. The sea turtle digs the egg chamber using her flippers.

Embryo—All babies come from embryos—that's the same for sea turtles and humans! An embryo is a collection of divided cells which eventually make cute hatchlings.

Emergence—sea turtle hatchlings break free of their egg using one long tooth called a caruncle. They have to work hard to be born! Baby sea turtles follow a source of light and try to outrun predators to reach the ocean waves. Also see Caruncle.

Endotherm—humans regulate their own body temperature, so we are endothermic, or warm-blooded. Sea turtles are ectothermic, or cold-blooded, so they are affected by their surroundings, with the exception of Leatherback Turtles, who have some ability to regulate their own body temperature, so they are slightly endothermic. Green Sea Turtles can also do this to a less extent.

Extinction—some species of animals die out (they no longer exist) because of catastrophic events or changes to their environment (like the dinosaurs). Sea turtles are being killed by human beings, and are in danger of dying out. You may not be sad that T-rex's aren't walking the streets of your town, but imagine if sea turtles were no longer around!

False Crawl—sea turtles 'crawl' across beaches to lay their eggs, but frequently they fail to deposit their eggs in the nest, often because they are disorientated by artificial lighting. Instead, the female sea turtle might accidentally deposit her eggs back in the ocean, where the eggs won't develop into hatchlings.

Feeding Grounds—Sea turtles like to eat near reefs, and near the coastline. They have established places they like to eat (like you or I having a favorite restaurant). They migrate to their favorite eateries.

Fibropapilloma—sea turtles suffer from this disease which causes tumors to develop all over their bodies, and affects their senses, and their organs. It can be fatal.

Flatback Turtle—these sea turtles can be spotted off the coast of Australia, where they nest.

Flipper—a sea turtle uses their flippers to swim, dig a body pit, and to excavate the egg chamber. Flippers are the sea turtle equivalent of arms and legs!

Foraging—sea turtles have to search for their food. Humans can go to fast food restaurants, but turtles must hunt, and usually migrate to feeding grounds where they can find their favorite food.

Gelatinivore—sea turtles enjoy eating jelly too, but they like their jelly salty, alive and kicking! Gelatinivore is an animal that likes eating jelly fish.

Green Turtle—the most common sea turtle, they are herbivores, and they are usually brown or gray in color.

Habitat—a habitat is a home, but sea turtles don't have one home, they have many. The entire ocean and our shorelines is 'home' to these ocean-dwelling creatures.

Hatchling—a baby sea turtle that has just broken free of its egg.

Hawksbill Turtle—one of the most endangered sea turtle species. Enjoys hanging out in coral reefs, is easy to identify because of its hawk-like pointy snout or 'bill' and its shell is highly prized for its patterned amber shell.

Herbivore—a creature that enjoys eating vegetables!

Honu—the Hawaiian word for sea turtle.

Incubation—the time it takes sea turtle embryos to develop in their eggs. Temperature affects the duration of incubation.

Invertebrate—sea turtles can't grow a backbone because they don't have spines! So they known as invertebrates.

Juvenile—a young turtle (like a teenager!).

Kemp's Ridley Turtle—there are very few of these turtles left, and they nest mainly in Rancho Nuevo, Mexico.

Leatherback Turtle—the biggest turtle of them all, it has a leathery shell. They love jellyfish!

Loggerhead Turtle—likes to crunch food with its oversized jaw. Favorite food: mollusks and vegetables.

Longline—a huge fishing net that poses a danger to sea turtles who get caught on the baited hooks.

Marine Protected Area—protected areas of ocean and beaches that are watched and managed to give sea turtles and other animals a better chance of survival.

Migration—sea turtles travel huge distances to feed, nest and mate.

Navigation—sea turtles are the Kings of Navigation. They can find their way no matter where they are in the world. They never need to stop and ask for directions.

Nest—where sea turtles lay their eggs and hatchlings are born. Nests are laid on beaches.

Nocturnal—creatures who like to stay up all night. Sea turtles mainly like to be active during the day, but they use the cover of night to nest and hatch.

Olive Ridley Turtle—this turtle likes to sunbathe in hot countries near the equator, like India and Mexico.

Omnivore—creatures with a well-rounded diet. Omnivores eat anything—meat or vegetables.

Orientation—sea turtles figure out their position on the earth using the sun and moon. They don't need a GPS to figure out where they are.

Overfishing—when fishermen catch too many fish, there isn't enough time for more baby fish to be born, so the number of fish in the ocean declines.

Plastron—the lower shell (belly area) of the turtle.

Pollution—toxic substances in the environment that have a negative effect on sea turtles and other creatures.

Predator—creatures that hunt and eat other creatures or plants.

Preservation—many environments are in danger from human interaction or climate change. Preservation is the act of protecting these areas.

Relocation (of nests)—volunteers sometimes relocate sea turtle nests if they are in danger from the tide, humans or sea turtles.

Scales—Sea turtles are reptiles, so they have 'plates' that overlap and protect their skin.

Scutes—similar to scales, scutes are part of a turtle's shell and offer protection.

Sexual Maturity—when sea turtles are at an age to start mating and reproducing. This varies between 3 and 50 years old, depending on the sea turtle!

Species—a way of classifying different types of creatures, depending on their type, origin and breeding habits.

Spongivore—an animal that eats sponges (like the Hawksbill Turtle).

Sustainability—a population is sustainable if it can replenish its population.

Tagging—sea turtles are tagged by humans with tracking devices, so we can track and study their movements and habits throughout their lives. There are different types of tags.

Tracking—see Tagging.

Trawler—a type of fishing net that is cast and towed along the bottom of the ocean. Turtle Excluder Device (TED)—these devices allow sea turtles to escape from fishing nets.

Ventral—see Plastron.

Other Great Books by
Stephanie Lisa Tara

Snowy White World
to Save

USA BEST BOOK
AWARDS
FINALIST
USABookNews.com

Story by Stephanie Lisa Tara
Illustrations by Alex Walton

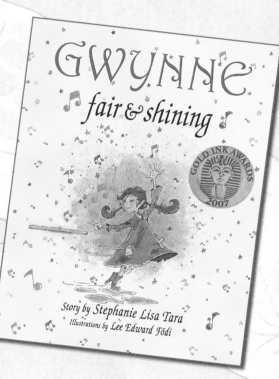

GWYNNE
fair & shining

GOLD INK AWARDS
2007

Story by Stephanie Lisa Tara
Illustrations by Lee Edward Födi

MOM'S CHOICE AWARDS
HONORING EXCELLENCE

Eliza's
Forever
Trees

"Enchanting story . . . the writing lyrical:
'Great Mother Redwood had always been
here, always watching and protecting,
guarding her family—as all mothers do.'"
—Ricki Lewis, PhD
Geneticist, author, mom

Stephanie Lisa Tara
Author of international bestseller I'll Follow the Moon

Start

Flip Back

Made in the USA
San Bernardino, CA
02 June 2013